LifeChange

A NAVPRESS BIBLE STUDY SERIES

*A life-changing encounter with God's Word*

# ANXIETY

*God's presence meets us in our struggles, guiding us from anxious striving to deep trust.*



NavPress

Published in alliance with Tyndale House Publishers

NavPress
Bold. Loving. Sensible.

NavPress.com

*Anxiety: A Bible Study on Finding Peace in God's Presence*



A NavPress resource published in alliance with Tyndale House Publishers



Written by Janae Collins

The Team:
David Zimmerman, Publisher; Caitlyn Carlson, Acquisitions Editor; Lisa Schrad, Developmental Editor; Elizabeth Schroll, Copyeditor; Lacie Phillips, Production Assistant; Ellery Sterling, Designer; Sarah Ocenasek, Proofreading Coordinator



For information about special discounts for bulk purchases, please contact Tyndale House Publishers at csresponse@tyndale.com, or call 1-855-277-9400.

ISBN 978-1-64158-970-3

Printed in the United States of America

32 31 30 29 28 27 26
7 6 5 4 3 2

*This is dedicated to Jesus and my husband, who have both shown me the beauty of God's presence within my own anxiety.*

*Janae Collins*

# CONTENTS

# HOW TO USE THIS STUDY

## Objectives

The topical guides in the LifeChange series of Bible studies cover important topics from the Bible. Although the LifeChange guides vary with the topics they explore, they share some common goals:

1. to help readers grasp what key passages in the Bible say about the topic;
2. to provide readers with explanatory notes, word definitions, historical background, and cross-references so that the only other reference they need is the Bible;
3. to teach readers how to let God's Word transform them into Christ's image;
4. to provide small groups with a tool that will enhance group discussion of each passage and topic; and
5. to write each session so that advance preparation for group members is strongly encouraged but not required.

Each lesson in this study is designed to take forty-five minutes to complete.

## Overview and Details

The study begins with an overview of anxiety. The key to interpretation for each part of this study is content (what is the referenced passage *about*?), and the key to context is purpose (what is the author's *aim* for the passage as it relates to the overall topic?). The individual lessons of the study each explore a person from Scripture who experienced some kind of anxiety and offer corresponding passages from the Bible that point us to God's compassion and invitations in the midst of it.

## Kinds of Questions

Bible study provides different lenses and perspectives through which to engage the Scripture: observe (what does the passage *say*?), interpret (what does the passage *mean*?), and apply (how does this truth *affect* my life?). Some of the "how" and "why" questions will take some creative thinking, even prayer, to answer. Some are opinion questions without clear-cut right answers; these will lend themselves to discussions and side studies.

Don't let your study become an exercise in knowledge alone. Treat the passage as God's Word, and stay in dialogue with Him as you study. Pray, *Lord, what do You want me to see here?, Father, why is this true?,* and *Lord, how does this apply to my life?*

It is important that you write down your answers. The act of writing clarifies your thinking and helps you remember what you're learning.

## Study Aids

Throughout the guide, there are study aids that provide background information on the passage, insights from commentaries, and word studies. These aids are included in the guide to help you interpret the Bible without needing to use outside resources. Still, if you're interested in exploring further, the full resources are listed in the endnotes.

## Scripture Versions

Unless otherwise indicated, the Bible quotations in this guide are from the English Standard Version of the Bible (ESV). Other versions cited are the Christian Standard Bible (CSB), the King James Version (KJV), *The Message* (MSG), the New International Version (NIV), and the New Living Translation (NLT).

Use any translation you like for study—or preferably more than one. Ideally you would have on hand a good modern translation, such as the New International Version, the English Standard Version, the New Living Translation, or the Christian Standard Bible. It can also be helpful to consult a thought-for-thought translation, such as *The Message*.

## Memorizing and Meditating

A psalmist wrote, "I have hidden your word in my heart that I might not sin against you" (Psalm 119:11, NIV). If you write down a verse or passage that challenges or encourages you and reflect on it often for a week or more, you will find it beginning to affect your motives and actions. We forget quickly what we read once; we remember what we ponder.

When you find a significant verse or passage, you might copy it onto a card to keep with you. Set aside five minutes each day just to think about what the passage might mean in your life. Recite it to yourself, exploring its meaning. Then, return to the passage as often as you can during the day for a brief review. You will soon find it coming to mind spontaneously.

## For Group Study

A group of four to ten people allows for the richest discussions, but you can adapt this guide for other-sized groups. It will suit a wide range of group types, such as home Bible studies, growth groups, youth groups, and workplace Bible studies. Both new and experienced Bible students, and new and mature Christians, will benefit from the guide. You can omit or leave for later any questions you find too easy or too hard.

The guide is intended to lead a group through one lesson per meeting. This guide is formatted so you will be able to discuss each of the questions at length. Be sure to make time at each discussion for members to ask about anything they didn't understand.

Each member should prepare for a meeting by writing answers for all the background and discussion questions to be covered. Application will be very difficult, however, without private thought and prayer.

Two reasons for studying in a group are accountability and support. When each member commits in front of the rest to seek growth in an area of life, you can pray for one another, listen jointly for God's guidance, help one another resist temptation, assure each other that each person's growth matters to you, use the group to practice spiritual principles, and so on. Pray about one another's commitments and needs at most meetings. If you wish, you can spend the first few minutes of each meeting sharing any results from applications prompted by previous lessons and discuss new applications toward the end of the meeting. Follow your time of sharing with prayer for these and other needs.

If you write down what others have shared, you are more likely to remember to pray for them during the week, ask about what they shared at the next meeting, and notice answered prayers. You might want to get a notebook for prayer requests and discussion notes.

Taking notes during discussion will help you remember to follow up on ideas, stay on the subject, and have clarity on an issue. But don't let note-taking keep you from participating.

Some best practices for groups:

1. If possible, come to the group discussion prepared. The more each group member knows about the passage and the questions being asked, the better your discussion will be.
2. Realize that the group leader will not be teaching from the passage but instead will be facilitating your discussion. Therefore, it is important for each group member to participate so that everyone can contribute to what you learn as a group.
3. Try to stick to the passage covered in the session and the specific questions in the study guide.

4. Listen attentively to the other members of the group when they are sharing their thoughts about the passage. Also realize that most of the questions are open-ended, allowing for more than one answer.
5. Be careful not to dominate the discussion—especially if you are the leader. Allow time for everyone to share their thoughts and ideas.
6. As mentioned previously, throughout the session are study aids that provide background information on the passage, insights from commentaries, and word studies. Reading these aloud during the meeting is optional and up to the discussion leader. However, each member can refer to these insights if they found them helpful in understanding the passage.

## A Note on Topical Studies

LifeChange guides offer robust and thoughtful engagement with God's Word. The book-centric guides focus on a step-by-step walk through that particular book of the Bible. The topical studies use Scripture to help you engage more deeply with God's Word and its implications for your life.

# INTRODUCTION

## Anxiety

ASK TWENTY-FIVE PEOPLE about their personal experience with anxiety, and you will likely receive twenty-five different answers. This has the potential to be beautiful: It points to a creative God and the unique ways He made us. But it can also be deeply frustrating to struggle to find common ground with others who experience anxiety. Anxiety isn't easily placed in a tidy box or prescribed a cure for. It is messy, difficult, and confusing. And it has a leading role in our culture: In a recent Household Pulse Survey conducted by the US Census Bureau, approximately one-third of adults surveyed reported experiencing symptoms of anxiety or depression.[1]

In its most basic form, anxiety is the presence of worry. Feeling powerless unravels our fears. When our panic feels out of control or when our thoughts cannot stop spiraling, our bodies and actions reveal pent-up, hidden stresses. We are created by a sovereign God and given freedom by Him. However, as humans living in a broken world, we will be tempted to grasp for control instead of depending on God. Anxiety forms in us when we push back against the act of surrender. As beings who are created by a sovereign God *and* given freedom, we walk in a daily tension. In our human nature, we desire to pursue independence. But in our redeemed nature, our hearts are called to surrender to humility.

"Normal" anxiety—which often feels anything but normal—occurs when there is a specific stressful situation or problem in one's life. The anxious feelings will last through the process of finding a resolution to that situation. When anxiety creeps up unexpectedly, feels hard to control, and lasts for a longer time, it may be due to an anxiety disorder.[2]

Anxiety is often placed in the category of mental health, but it can be misunderstood as only a physical ailment, where panic attacks send you to the hospital questioning your life. Anxiety can look big and scary, and it can feel like an actual elephant is sitting on your chest. And it can also look like a sleepless night, an angry outburst in the parking lot, or your leg tapping uncontrollably in the school car line.

The world tends to focus on symptoms and quick fixes. Humans are tempted to grasp at anything that eases the lack of control or bitterness we experience. It is only through deep work (and sometimes outside help), however, that anxiety can move from being an enemy to being a friend. This deep work invites us to ask hard questions about ourselves to find the root that is producing branches of fear in our everyday lives.

Whether you or a loved one has wrestled with anxiety, this study is meant to meet you where you are. It holds six stories of people in the Bible who also understood the tameless fear of anxious experiences. From Martha and her desire for control to Jesus sweating blood in Gethsemane to Peter trying to overcome his own fear, people in the Bible show us how peace and anxiety can coexist with the power and presence of Jesus.

With a lot of patience and surrender, we can learn together that although anxiety is rooted in fear, it is not something to be feared in and of itself. It is a beautiful open door to a deeper relationship with Jesus, and it is an intimate place to feel His presence. Knowing that Jesus Himself experienced anxiety, we can accept the invitation to confidently walk in His footsteps through the struggle, praising our good God, from whom all blessings flow.

*Session One*

# MARTHA AND ANXIOUS CONTROL

## Luke 10:38-42

HAVE YOU EVER WANTED to be seen so badly that the worst parts of you have come out toward the least-deserving people? Maybe you've studied for eight hours for a final exam, fighting the sleep that called your name, only to get the same grade as your roommate, who didn't study. As a result, you take your anger out on them the next time you see them. Or maybe you and your spouse are arguing about who is more tired that day or who did more chores that week and you go to sleep fighting. Maybe, like Martha, you go out of your way to make sure you are seen for your actions because you'll feel inadequate if you don't. But in doing so, you make snide remarks to anyone who gets in your way or messes up your plans.

Martha is most known for her frustration and her focus on hospitality. She's never the person women (or men) want to be like. Her tunnel vision was bent toward serving, responding, and doing. Though sermons about this Scripture passage tend to focus on her sister, Mary, let's expend some empathy for Martha. As likely the oldest sibling of Mary and Lazarus,[1] she held on to more responsibility than they did in her household. It's safe to assume she craved depth and connection but came off as stressed and controlling instead. She carried the weight of welcoming guests into her home and managing their experiences and expectations.

Martha's identity proved to be rooted in pleasing: She yearned for Jesus to perceive her as "enough" by the appearance of her home and the quality of the meal she prepared. This desire to control people and situations is a familiar one.

In the story we'll read, we also see Martha's sister sitting at the feet of Jesus. This was a formal posture in the first century, reserved for recognized disciples. And people didn't include women or invite them into this posture—until Jesus.[2] Martha, already anxious about her home, seems to be tempted to control her sister's behavior with Rabbi Jesus as well. This is a big day with a special guest, and it is her time to shine. But Martha's anxiety gives her a narrow perspective, and she begins acting out of her lack of control over the situation. She trusts her need to please and perfect instead of trusting what Jesus can offer her. Tightening her grip on the home, Martha complains to Jesus about her sister's inattention to what seems most important and fails to see the presence of Jesus before her.

But Jesus gives her another chance. And instead of rolling His eyes and whispering judgmental comments with Mary in the corner, Jesus makes eye contact with Martha, gently says her name, and invites her into His presence of peace.

Bible teacher Jennie Allen writes, "When Jesus walked the earth, story after story of His ministry confirmed how He cared about each person He came across. He cared about their mind. He cared about their body. He cared about their soul. He even cared about their emotions."[3]

---

1. Read Luke 10:38-42. What do you think would make Martha's list of worries?

2. How did Martha's worries differ from her sister's?

3. What are three things that would currently make your list of worries?

"Breathing a prayer to God is a simple way of using your body to engage your mind on the Word of God. Whispering the words of Scripture as you are breathing in and out, slowly and deeply, over and over, can help you to 'abide' in Christ (John 15:4, 5, 9)."[4]

Practice: Try this breath prayer based on Psalm 23:1.

Breathe in: *The Lord is my shepherd.*

Breathe out: *I have everything that I need.*

4. In Martha's culture, maintaining and running a home was the epitome of a woman's identity. Keeping this in mind, what can we conclude about Martha's actions and heart?

5. In what situations do you, like Martha, tend to try to alleviate your anxiety by taking control? How have you resonated with Martha's worry over hosting others or caring for your family members?

6. Read Luke 10:39 once more. What is Mary doing?

7. Since women weren't yet invited to sit at the feet of rabbis in the first century, what additional fears might Mary's actions have raised for Martha underneath her controlling behavior?

"What Martha was doing was providing hospitality and welcome, and this was vitally important in the culture of the time. In first-century Palestine, hospitality was (and still is) about allowing the guest to share the sacredness of the family space. The women's role was (and still is in many households) to do the cooking and food preparation. Martha was doing just what was expected of her.

"What was unexpected was what Mary was doing.

"It was very unusual for Jewish Palestinian women to join male guests before they are done with all the food preparation. And even more unusual for a woman to be sitting amongst the men in the posture of a disciple."[5]

8. What was Jesus' posture toward Martha? What were his words to her? Why were these significant for her anxiety and her desire for control?

"It is easy to look at all we do and to criticize those who don't seem to do as much. But Martha's real problem wasn't Mary; it was Martha. She had become distracted and had taken her eyes off Jesus.

"Martha's frustration is typical of those who diligently serve with good intent, but forget to *also* sit at Jesus' feet."[6]

9. Consider whether you've ever met someone like Martha. If so, what has been your posture toward them? If not, how do you imagine you might respond to them?

10. When have you experienced Jesus' redirection of your gaze and the calming presence of His peace when you've been focused on controlling good things but missing the best thing? Did you notice a shift in your anxiety and desire to control?

The phenomenon of encountering our smallness is called unselfing. Author Hannah Brencher explains, "Unselfing is what happens when we turn away from ourselves and look outward. Our bodies react in pretty miraculous ways. Our nervous system calms down, and there's a release of oxytocin—the chemical that stirs up feelings of love and trust within us. We feel more connected to others. Our worries hush. Our mental chatter grows quieter. We become less self-absorbed."[7]

## Your Response

We could focus on many things today, but only one is needed. How do the following verses address your tendency to grasp for control? Which passage meets you most where you are today?

Matthew 6:25-34

Luke 21:33-34

Philippians 4:6-7

## For Further Study

We meet Martha again in John 11. Take time to read John 11:17-32. How has Martha grown here? How is her inner anxiety and desire for control displaying itself?

*Session Two*

# KING SAUL AND ANXIOUS ENVY

## 1 Samuel 18:6-16, 25-30

WHEN WAS THE LAST TIME you felt jealous of someone? Did that envy take root in your life and affect those around you? Was there room for God to enter your thoughts?

As one article puts it, "*Envy lies. It tells us that others have better homes, jobs, partners and personalities.* It casts a long shadow over one's own accomplishments and tells us that others have done more and better. Envy in and of itself is an unpleasant feeling, but when coupled with depression and anxiety, it can become a toxic combination."[1]

Envy has been a common human experience since the fall, and we see it clearly displayed in Saul, Israel's first king, as part of his anxiety. The son of a prominent man of the tribe of Benjamin, Saul was "impressive among the Israelites" (1 Samuel 9:2, CSB). He had no leadership experience, but Saul was chosen by God and anointed by Samuel to lead Israel: "Then Samuel took a flask of olive oil and poured it on Saul's head and kissed him, saying, 'Has not the LORD anointed you ruler over his inheritance?'" (1 Samuel 10:1, NIV).

Imagine being the first person to hold this position.

After being found hiding in the back of the crowd with insecurity evident on his face, Saul was given a chance at new freedom and power. A new calling. This ultimately led him in his leadership to defeat enemies, but the position also came at a cost—it brought with it the temptation for pride and envy.

As king, Saul became insecure, angry, and jealous that the shepherd boy David, whom he had once deeply loved (1 Samuel 16:21), was consistently successful in his pursuits and getting glory instead of him. Eventually his envy became all-consuming. Dinners became opportunities to attempt murder, and Saul even made a strategic family alliance between his daughter and David in an attempt to trip up his young rival: "By offering Michal [in marriage], Saul appeared generous, yet he intended to entangle David politically and militarily."[2] Saul's lack of attunement to his envy and the anxiety that sprang from it only watered the seeds of resentment in his heart.

Eventually, "the LORD regretted that he had made Saul king over Israel" (1 Samuel 15:35) and "the Spirit of the LORD departed from Saul" (1 Samuel 16:14), leaving room for a harmful spirit to torment him. This caused an even deeper root of anxiety to form as Saul became jealous of the Lord's presence with David. Not only had Saul lost God's presence, but he had also lost his purpose and identity.

Pastor David Guzik explains, "David became popular because he was a *man after God's own heart* and people could see the *love*, the *wisdom*, and the *peace* of God in him."[3]

---

1. Read 1 Samuel 18:6-16. What do you notice about Saul's experience in this passage?

"Fear is experienced in your mind, but it triggers a strong physical reaction in your body.

"As soon as you recognize fear, your amygdala (small organ in the middle of your brain) goes to work. It alerts your nervous system, which sets your body's fear response into motion. . . .

"Your body releases stress hormones like cortisol and adrenaline. Your blood pressure and heart rate increase. You start breathing faster.

"Even your blood flow changes. Blood flows away from your heart and into your limbs, making it easier for you to start throwing punches or run for your life. Your body is preparing for a fight-or-flight response."[4]

2. Different translations use different words to describe Saul's fear in 1 Samuel 18:15 (emphasis added below). After reading the following, what do you notice?

    - "When Saul saw that he had great success, he stood in *fearful awe* of him."
    - "When Saul saw that he behaved himself very wisely, he was *afraid* of [David]" (KJV).
    - "When Saul recognized this, he became even *more afraid* of him" (NLT).
    - "As Saul saw David becoming more successful, he himself grew *more fearful*. He could see the handwriting on the wall" (MSG).
    - "When Saul observed that David was very successful, he *dreaded* him" (CSB).

3. Reread 1 Samuel 18:10-11, and read 1 Samuel 18:25-30. Up until this point, David has been a friend of Saul's who sings to him when darkness overtakes his spirit. How do you think David might feel at this turn of events?

"David sang to the mad king. . . .

"Nonetheless, the king was mad, and therefore he was jealous. Or was it the other way around? Either way, Saul felt threatened by David, as kings often do when there is a popular, promising young man beneath them. The king also knew, as did David, that this boy just might have his job some day."[5]

4. When you experience jealousy, what are the first things you feel, think, and experience?

5. One psychologist points out that jealousy "in extreme forms . . . can be toxic, and damaging to relationships."[6] Describe how Saul and David's relationship became damaged. What are some different actions each of them could have taken to avoid a broken relationship?

"[God] had already set [the Israelites] free from slavery. The commands were about helping them stay free and helping them flourish in their new life."[7]

6. In Exodus 20, God gives the Ten Commandments. Nine are outward or external commands about relating to people or God. Only one command focuses on an inward attitude: Do not envy (verse 17). Why do you think God includes this in His instructions to the Israelites (and us), and how does it relate to our anxious thoughts?

7. Contentment is something we all strive for, and we often mistakenly think we'll attain it through success, material possessions, and more. But God invites us into contentment and intimacy through a command to not be envious. In what ways have you struggled to find contentment in your current season of life?

"Godliness with contentment is great gain, for we brought nothing into the world, and we cannot take anything out of the world. But if we have food and clothing, with these we will be content" (1 Timothy 6:6-8).

8. How has anxiety expressed itself through discontentment in your story?

"Contentment is essential, and difficult for many reasons:

- "We can only find contentment when our hearts are rooted in eternal things; and contentment is essential because it shows we are living with an eternal perspective. . . .
- "It is hard to be content, because our consumer culture feeds our lack of contentment, by rewarding us when we are discontent, and with advertising that tries to make us feel discontent without a product.
- "It is hard to be content, because we almost always desire far more than we need."[8]

9. James 3:16 says, "Where jealousy and selfish ambition exist, there will be disorder and every vile practice." What is one way you could respond in a healthy manner to moments of jealousy or selfish ambition?

"Jesus said that the first and great commandment is to love the Lord your God. 'You *shall* [it's a command] love the Lord your God with all your heart' (Matthew 22:37). *All of it.* 'With all your heart,' God demands that we love him. 'Don't give any of your affections that belong to God to anyone else,' he's saying. Or the way the Old Testament put it in Exodus 34:14: 'You shall worship'—that is, treasure, reverence, admire, esteem, praise, love, delight in—'no other god, for the Lord, whose name is Jealous, is a jealous God.'"[9]

10. Throughout Scripture, God is known as a jealous God (e.g., Exodus 20:5; 34:14; Deuteronomy 4:24). Read 2 Corinthians 11:2. How does God's jealousy differ from Saul's anxious jealousy?

## Your Response

Fear, insecurity, self-image issues, anxiety, depression, and past trauma can cause persistent jealousy. Describe a time you've felt these feelings take over your body and mind. What are a few practical steps you can take to help you step out of the downward cycle of persistent jealousy?

Tim Mackie and Aeron Sullivan reflect, "Unlike Saul, Jesus was a king of Israel who never failed, but took upon himself the consequences of the failure of others. Unlike Saul, Jesus never flinched when faced with the dark side of humanity. Rather, he ran directly into it with his love and passion because he knew that God's power could overcome our evil and create something new. What Saul needed, and what we really need, are new hearts and minds that don't need to defend themselves or justify failure and selfishness."[10]

## For Further Study

The story of Israel's first king is about how unaddressed anxiety breeds toxic jealousy. Look at 1 Samuel 9:3-5 and 10:2. Who is struggling with anxiety in these passages? How might that have set a mark on Saul's story? How have your family dynamics been affected by jealousy in your own story?

*Session Three*

# JESUS AND EMBODIED ANXIETY

## Luke 22:7-53

*Hematohidrosis* IS NOT A WORD used daily by most people. An article on the National Library of Medicine's website defines it as a rare clinical phenomenon occurring when "severe mental anxiety activates the sympathetic nervous system to invoke stress-fight reaction to such a degree as to cause hemorrhage of the vessels supplying the sweat glands into the ducts of the sweat glands."[1] In other words, feelings of panic, anxiety, and anguish can cause a person to sweat blood.

It is one thing to read the Gospel stories about Jesus and admire His complete deity. He performs miracles, He is God incarnate, He is sinless, and He is good. He is where we find satisfaction, restoration, redemption, and steadfast love and kindness.

It is something entirely different to believe that Jesus is also fully human. He grew up learning the trade of carpentry with His dad, He had a loving relationship with His mom, He knew illnesses and scrapes and bruises from playing with His siblings, and He understood weariness from travel and heartache from broken relationships.

In the last hours before Jesus' crucifixion, after preparing His closest friends for something they couldn't understand yet and leading them to the garden of Gethsemane, Jesus "withdrew about a stone's throw beyond them, knelt down and prayed, 'Father, if you are willing, take this cup from me; yet not my will, but yours be done.' An angel from heaven appeared to him and strengthened him. And being in anguish, he prayed more earnestly, and his sweat was *like drops of blood falling to the ground*" (Luke 22:41-44, NIV, emphasis added).

Clearly the anguish and deep grief Jesus experienced affected His physical body—so much so that He fell down and prayed from His deepest anxiety for a way out. Jesus returned from this moment with His Father to find His disciples asleep. How immensely lonely He must've felt. His disciples didn't see Jesus or the weight He was carrying. Yet, as counselor and author K. J. Ramsey reflects, "Jesus kneeled on the ground of that garden, allowing himself to feel the utter depths of fear itself—anxiety so severe it made his sweat ducts bleed—so that there can be no depth of darkness we experience that is outside the reach of his empathy."[2]

There was and is immense purpose to this moment in Jesus' life.

---

1. Have you ever considered Jesus as someone who has experienced anxiety? Does this concept make you uncomfortable? Why or why not?

2. Read Luke 22:7-53. Write a short timeline of the events described there.

"Jesus drew upon the prophecies of Jeremiah (31:31-34) concerning the new covenant that God would make with his people and solemnly pointed out that the time had arrived. His blood about to be shed was the blood of the covenant, symbolized by the wine, and his body about to be broken was symbolized by the bread (Mt 26:26-29)."[3]

3. Look back at your timeline. What emotions do you perceive from Jesus during these events?

4. Which emotion do you resonate with the most today, and why?

5. Jesus was "despised and rejected by mankind, a man of suffering, and familiar with pain" (Isaiah 53:3, NIV). Jesus knew every prophecy written about Him and that His purpose on earth was to fulfill them. Why do you think He still prayed for a way out?

"Crucifixion was a powerful symbol throughout the Roman world. It was not just a means of liquidating undesirables; it did so with maximum degradation and humiliation. It said, loud and clear: we are in charge here; you are our property; we can do what we like with you. It insisted, coldly and brutally, on the absolute sovereignty of Rome, and of Caesar."[4]

6. The Father heard Jesus' pleading cry in the garden, but the Bible doesn't say that He took away Jesus' anxious feelings. We do know that God did not respond by changing the outcome of that weekend. How does the posture of Jesus pleading in the garden resonate with your own anxious prayers?

7. Read Hebrews 4:15-16. What stands out to you most from these verses related to Jesus' embodied anxiety?

8. Jesus chose to experience a life that promised Him grief, hardship, and ultimately death. What do you admire most about Jesus as He walked through anxiety in the garden?

9. The Greek word *perilypos* is used in Matthew 26:38, where Jesus tells His disciples that He is "deeply grieved" (CSB). It can also be translated "grieved all around," "intensely sad," or "exceedingly sorrowful."[5] Have you ever felt swallowed up in sorrow, grieved all around? Consider taking a moment to name the experience and invite your High Priest into it with you.

"Jesus went to his death knowing that it was his Father's will that he face death completely alone ([Matthew] 27:46) as the sacrificial, wrath-averting Passover Lamb. As his death was unique, so also his anguish; and our best response to it is hushed worship."[6]

10. It was necessary for Jesus to suffer anguish and anxiety in the garden without receiving the answers He was asking for. And in so doing, He revealed the depths of His humanity and ability to relate with us. Read John 16:31-33. What truth was Jesus carrying with Him through His last week on earth before His crucifixion?

"Jesus was distressed at the spiritual horror waiting for Him on the cross," David Guzik writes. "Jesus would stand in the place of guilty sinners and receive all the spiritual punishment sinners deserve; He *who knew no sin* would *be sin for us* (2 Corinthians 5:21)."[7]

"Our greatest hope for our bodies and minds facing every kind of battle with anxiety is Jesus."[8]

## Your Response

By dying on the cross and shedding His own blood, Jesus became our sacrifice. He is the High Priest, and we are His royal priesthood. How would you describe this to someone new in their faith? How does this reality speak to you in your own moments of anxiety or anguish?

## For Further Study

Author Alastair Roberts writes, "When God's dwelling with his people in the new Eden of the tabernacle was threatened by human trespass and corruption, he provided a Day of Atonement when communion might be graciously preserved through sacrifice. Yet, as Hebrews makes clear, the blood of bulls and goats does not take away sins. Christ is the One whose sacrifice truly cleanses the heavenly holy places, and he's the One who, like the scapegoat, utterly removes and bears away our sins."[9]

In your own words, how did Jesus' life replace the old system of atonement? Use Leviticus 16 and Hebrews 5:1-6 for reference.

*Session Four*

# NAOMI AND ANXIOUS BITTERNESS

## Ruth 1; 2:14-23; 4:14-17

ANXIETY DOES NOT ALWAYS PRESENT ITSELF in a physical way, such as in a panic attack with sweaty palms and a racing heartbeat. It can hide within deeper emotions and has the capacity to slow brew its way into our stories when we aren't looking. This means that, while it's not the sole cause of anger, anxiety can and does appear in many individuals as frustration, anger, and bitterness.

Psychologist Seth Meyers writes, "Emotional bitterness refers to feelings of sadness, resentment, and anger—especially anger—that accumulate over time. It is a secondary emotion, outside of sadness, happiness, fear, anger, surprise, and disgust, that can result from insult or injury. Feeling bitter involves mixed emotions, and it can be hard to identify and express in simple terms."[1] Meyers says, "Feeling bitter is the likely consequence of feeling invalidated and unappreciated in one too many situations and relationships."[2]

This is the state Naomi ended up in. Initially, she had a full life according to her culture's standards: a husband, a home, and sons who married, giving her the hope of future grandchildren. But when tragedy unexpectedly robbed Naomi of her husband and sons, the lie that she was unworthy, unloved, and unseen crept into her heart.

Naomi's resentment urged her to go so far as to make bitterness her name and her story. Loneliness can be a trigger for anxiety, easily encouraging us to sink into a victim mentality. God had insulted Naomi one too many times, and she was out. Upon returning home to her native country and people, she declared, "Do not call me Naomi; call me Mara, for the Almighty has dealt very bitterly with me. I went away full, and the LORD has brought me back empty. Why call me Naomi, when the LORD has testified against me and the Almighty has brought calamity upon me?" (Ruth 1:20-21).

But the God of Naomi is the God of us. He faithfully pursued her, rewriting her pain for her and bringing restoration and insight into His bigger plan for her. God not only gave her grace upon grace (see John 1:16) but He also refused to let bitterness be the end of her story. Naomi (which means "delight"[3]) was whom He had created, despite the brokenness and bitterness she was experiencing. And Naomi was the woman who, though walking a road of bitter anxiety and expressing that she felt defeated, held on to a deeper thread of faith in God's love for her people.

"Naomi didn't put on a false face. She wasn't going to go home, pretend everything was fine, and be 'pleasant.' She was honest and said, 'Here I am and my life has been bitter.'"[4]

---

1. Read Ruth 1. What do you notice about Naomi's relationship with the Lord and her relationship with Ruth?

2. Aubrey Sampson writes, "Our names can have the power to be badges of honor or badges of heartache. Adding to this emotional complexity, . . . we name or define ourselves in other ways, as well—by our jobs, marital statuses, roles, cultural contexts, ethnicities, Enneagram numbers, strengths, talents, spiritual gifts, religious affiliations, tribes, hobbies."[5] What emotions could have been affecting Naomi's decision to return home with a new name (Mara)?

3. What names have you given yourself in relation to your own anxiety?

The phrase "wonderfully made" in Psalm 139:14 comes from the Hebrew word *pālâ* , which can be defined as "to distinguish (literally or figuratively):—put a difference, show marvellous, separate, set apart, sever, make wonderfully."[6]

Bible commentator John Trapp reflects, "The greatest miracle in the world is man; in whose very body (how much more in his soul!) are miracles enough (between head and feet) to fill a volume."[7]

4. Bitter feelings quickly turn into resentment toward others. Naomi's bitterness was directed toward God, and she was not afraid to express it. Has anxiety shown up as bitter thoughts toward God in your life? If so, have you felt safe to express those thoughts to Him? What has that looked like?

"At Marah [the Israelites] had water, but it was bitter, so that though they had been three days without water they could not drink it, because it was extremely unpleasant to the taste or was likely to be prejudicial to their health, or was so brackish that it rather increased their thirst than quenched it, [Exodus 15] v. 23. Note, God can embitter that to us from which we promise ourselves most satisfaction, and often does so in the wilderness of this world, that our wants and disappointments in the creature may drive us to the Creator, in whose favour alone true comfort is to be had. Now in this distress, the people fretted and quarrelled with Moses, as if he had done ill by them. *What shall we drink?* is all their clamour, v. 24. Note, The greatest joys and hopes are soon turned into the greatest griefs and fears with those that live by sense only, and not by faith."[8]

5. The word *Marah* shows up in Exodus when the Israelites camp near a spring of bitter water. According to Exodus 15:22-25, what happened to the water after Moses prayed?

6. By turning bitter water sweet, God affirmed His place in His people's stories as healer and overseer. Naomi likely knew this story and maintained hope in her healing God when she moved back home with Ruth. Read Ruth 2:14-23. What words does Naomi use to describe God?

7. Read Ruth 4:14-17. What has happened in Naomi's story?

8. Though bitter feelings overtook Naomi's thoughts, she didn't stop trusting in her God. Had she allowed bitterness to take root, keeping her stuck without faith to move forward and grow, how might the familial storyline of Jesus have changed? (See Ruth 4:17.)

"Studies show that compassion protects against stress, anxiety, and depression. As compassion grows in us, it increases our empathy—it supports us in becoming more connected. It shifts our focus from self-centeredness to selflessness."[9]

9. In what ways do you see your story with God intertwined with Naomi's story with God? Bitterness tells a lie that life revolves around self, dimming hope in a good God. If you struggle with bitterness, what is it rooted in? Whom is it directed toward?

10. What hope do you find in the way God met Naomi in her story of anxious bitterness? Consider reading Ruth 3–4 to help better understand God's character.

"It was fitting that these blessings [God's provision of a kinsman-redeemer and a grandson] in the life of Naomi be given so much attention at the end of the book [of Ruth]. Naomi was the one whose original returning to the LORD began all this great work of God. If Naomi had not decided to go back to Bethlehem, the land of Israel, and the God of Israel, none of this would have happened."[10]

## Your Response

Consider someone you have not allowed yourself to fully forgive. How has this unforgiveness caused anxiety in your life? What is one step you can take this week toward releasing bitterness from your heart and inviting forgiveness in?

## For Further Study

To paraphrase is to put something into our own words to help our understanding or application of it. Paraphrase 2 Timothy 1:6-12 and underline any words that stand out. How can this passage help us counter our desire to remain bitter?

*Session Five*

# MOSES AND ANXIOUS AVOIDANCE

## Exodus 3:1–4:17

"God's concern for Israel frames Moses' encounter at the burning bush (Exod. 2:23-35 and 3:6-10). One image this literary frame creates is that of the bush representing Israel in the midst of fiery oppression in Egypt (cf. 'iron furnace' in Deut. 4:20; 1 Kgs. 8:51; Jer. 11:3-4). Though they are in the flames, they will not be consumed."[1]

AVOIDANCE IS ONE OF THE EASIEST, most common coping mechanisms for dealing with anxiety. It doesn't solve the problem itself, but it does offer a colorful Band-Aid while the initial fear settles. Take avoidance one step deeper and you find insecurity.

After surviving a murderous decree and the Nile River as a baby and then being returned to his birth mother to nurse, Moses grew up among the Egyptians. From the outside looking in generations later, we can clearly see that Moses had God's hand on him, guiding him to a specific purpose in years to come. But—like us—Moses didn't always see that and tried to avoid his calling multiple times. He fled after murdering an Egyptian, finding himself a quiet life as a shepherd that he was willing to adopt for the rest of his life—until God called his name through a burning bush and empowered him with a new task.

Like a toddler or teenager who asks the same question over and over until they hear the answer they want, Moses kept questioning God's choice of him for the job of leading the Israelites out of Pharaoh's hand. Consider the following cycle of anxiety and avoidance in Moses' life.[2]

> **Step 1: Anxiety.** "These may be physical feelings, such as increased heart rate, or mental symptoms, such as racing or intrusive thoughts." Moses' first response to God's plan was to question his own worth and God's choice of him as a leader. "Who am I that I should go?" he asked God (Exodus 3:11).

**Step 2: Avoidance.** "You feel uncomfortable and want to make these feelings stop, so you 'avoid' the situation, person, or thing that's causing them." Moses needed signs from God to assure him that people would believe him, and he emphasized his own weaknesses in public speaking (Exodus 4:1-10).

**Step 3: Relief.** Relief comes "by avoiding the situation that causes fear and anxiety." Symptoms are minimized, "but only for a short time." Moses was given relief when the Lord appointed Moses' brother Aaron as the public speaker for the two of them (Exodus 4:14-16).

**Step 4: Reinforcement.** "You've now taught your brain that you can't handle this anxiety or fear, which decreases your self-confidence, increases your anxiety, and leads to more avoidance." After not seeing immediate deliverance of the Israelites from Pharaoh, Moses became frustrated with the Lord and began to spiral again, asking, "Why, Lord, why have you brought trouble on this people? Is this why you sent me? . . . You have not rescued your people at all" (Exodus 5:22-23, NIV).

The Lord was compassionate, however—patient with Moses' insecurities and doubts—and steadfast in His plan to rescue His people from slavery. Though "the LORD's anger burned against Moses" (Exodus 4:14, NIV), God countered Moses' insecurity and avoidance with the truth of who God is, what He had done, and what He would do. For Moses the antidote to insecurity was trust. And often the antidote for our own insecurities and avoidance anxiety is also trust, not simply the disappearance of the issue.

---

"Far from his home, shepherding a flock at the foot of a mountain, Moses learns that his destiny is to shepherd another flock to the foot of Mount Horeb. God has indeed set him apart to deliver his people from Egypt. But despite the Lord's assurances, Moses' doubts persist."[3]

1. Look at the following timeline of events in Moses' life. How do you notice God providing for and leading Moses?

   a. Moses was adopted by Pharaoh's daughter, who found him floating in a basket on the Nile (Exodus 2:1-6).

   b. Moses was given to his birth mom to nurse (Exodus 2:7-10).

   c. Moses fled from Pharaoh after murdering an Egyptian, successfully escaping to Midian (Exodus 2:11-15).

d. God appeared to Moses in a burning bush and told him he would lead the Israelites out of slavery (Exodus 3:1–4:9).

e. Moses responded that he was not an eloquent speaker, and God said Aaron could speak to the Israelites for Moses (Exodus 4:10-17).

f. Moses and Aaron asked Pharaoh to free the Israelites. When he refused, they continued to listen to God throughout the plagues, trusting His strength instead of fearing Pharaoh's hardness of heart (Exodus 7–11).

g. Pharaoh freed the Israelites, and Moses led God's people safely through the Red Sea, while their Egyptian pursuers perished (Exodus 14).

2. Read Exodus 3:1–4:17. In your own words, describe the scene portrayed in these chapters. What part stands out to you most?

"**Ex. 3:14 I am who I am**. The three occurrences of 'I am' in v. 14 are all forms of the Hebrew verb 'to be.' Each relates to the divine name Yahweh ('the LORD' . . .). The word translated 'I am' can also be translated 'I will be.' . . . Given the context of v. 12 ('I will be with you'), the name of Yahweh ('the LORD') is a clear reminder of God's faithfulness to his people."[4]

"[Moses'] story isn't so much about a burning bush but about the Living God who refuses to look away," Professor Kristi McLelland explains. "He chooses to see, to hear, to let it matter—to let it all matter. And it's about the Living God who isn't afraid to come down, get in the middle of the ruins of this world, and put His hands all over them to restore us. We run from drama. The Lord runs into it to bring rescue, restoration, and renewal."[5]

3. God revealed His heart to Moses before He laid out His purpose for him, saying, "I have indeed seen the misery of my people. . . . I have heard them crying out because of their slave drivers, and I am concerned about their suffering. So I have come down to rescue them . . . and to bring them up out of that land [Egypt] into a good and spacious land. . . . The cry of the Israelites has reached me" (Exodus 3:7-9, NIV). What was God doing for Moses here?

4. Look back at the ways Moses revealed his desire to avoid God's calling (see the four-step avoidance cycle on pages 40–41). Which step is most intriguing to you? In what ways did Moses show his desire to avoid God's calling?

5. When we experience insecurity and a desire to avoid everything and everyone at all costs, God does not offer us a foolproof, fix-all plan. What was God's kind and simple response to Moses in Exodus 3:14?

_______________________________________________

_______________________________________________

_______________________________________________

_______________________________________________

_______________________________________________

_______________________________________________

_______________________________________________

6. The word *remember* occurs over two hundred times in the Bible. Read Genesis 9:16. What truth about God might Moses have been remembering? What was God calling Moses to remember about Him to settle his anxious thoughts? What are a few promises from God that you hold on to in your life?

_______________________________________________

_______________________________________________

_______________________________________________

_______________________________________________

_______________________________________________

_______________________________________________

_______________________________________________

_______________________________________________

_______________________________________________

_______________________________________________

_______________________________________________

_______________________________________________

_______________________________________________

"He is Emmanuel, God *with us*, the God who reminds his people over and over that [he] will be their God and they will be his people (Gen. 17:7; Ezek. 36:28; Jer. 7:23; 30:22). He is the God who walks *with us* in the darkness; he doesn't make our conquering of our own fears or darkness the contingency on which he works. He invites us to be strong and courageous *in himself*, trusting him to his promise."[6]

David Guzik writes: "Moses told the people of Israel to *stop*. This is often the LORD's direction to the believer in a time of crisis. *Despair* will cast you down, keeping you from standing. *Fear* will tell you to retreat. *Impatience* will tell you to do something now. *Presumption* will tell you to jump into the Red Sea before it is parted. Yet as God told Israel He often tells us to simply **stand still** and **hold your peace** as He reveals His plan."[7]

7. The strengthening of Moses' faith over and over through God's hardening of Pharaoh's heart prepared Moses to lead the Israelites to freedom. What words did Moses encourage the Israelites with as they were running in fear? (See Exodus 14:10-14.)

"*Salvation* is used [in Exodus 14:13] in its literal sense of saving life, or of victory instead of defeat in war. . . . As the Old Testament moves on, 'salvation' will gain a more spiritual and less material sense (Ps. 51:12), although the Hebrew was not conscious of any sharp contrast between the two."[8]

8. What effect does the truth of Exodus 14:14 have on your own insecurities, avoidance tendencies, and anxiety?

9. When have you experienced God calling you to trust Him? Were you prone to doubt God's voice at first?

10. Read Ephesians 1:3-10. What qualifies us to be called into ministry with God?

"These are components in the overarching realities of God's grace and glory. Father, Son, and Holy Spirit are alike active in bestowing divine favor on unworthy sinners. Paul prays for these truths to enlighten his readers ([Ephesians] 1:18), giving them strength like that which raised Christ from the dead and elevated him to God's right hand (1:20)."[9]

## Your Response

Look back at the cycle of anxiety and avoidance on pages 40–41. Take a moment to reflect on your own avoidance-anxiety tendencies and then write about a scenario from your life that demonstrates them. Take a few moments to lay your cycle before the Lord and ask Him for wisdom.

## For Further Study

Create a list of practical ways you could incorporate more gratitude into your daily routine.

First Peter 5:6-10 gives encouragement for anxiety that takes the form of insecurity and avoidance. If he could have had access to it, how might this passage have encouraged Moses in his specific circumstances? How does this passage bring hope to you today?

"By reducing the stress hormones and managing the autonomic nervous system functions, gratitude significantly reduces symptoms of depression and anxiety. At the neurochemical level, feelings of gratitude are associated with an increase in the neural modulation of the prefrontal cortex, the brain site responsible for managing negative emotions like guilt, shame, and violence."[10]

*Session Six*

# PETER AND ANXIETY ABOUT THE FUTURE

## John 18:15-18, 25-27; 21

WHAT COMES TO MIND when you think of the apostle Peter?

Simon Peter is a favorite person in the Bible for a lot of people due to his relatability. His fire for following Jesus matched his doubt, which can be true for many of us. Peter's life is proof of God's grace and gives a new perspective on God's qualifications for being a disciple. Following Jesus *includes* our humanity and our mess. Peter knew this well.

The biggest fear we see Peter face is the possibility of suffering. After a confusing dinner with Jesus, during which He washed His disciples' feet and they shared the last supper, Peter witnessed Jesus announce a betrayal from Judas and denouncement from him (John 13). After falling asleep in exhaustion, Peter then witnessed Jesus' arrest in the garden of Gethsemane.

Within twenty-four hours, Peter went from telling Jesus how much he loved Him and that he would never doubt Him to telling three different people or groups that he didn't know Jesus. Why? Because he didn't want to join Jesus in being persecuted. Even if he didn't know at this point that Jesus' trial would end in crucifixion, he was likely worried about his own family and future. Peter was probably also terrified of losing Jesus, his leader and friend. We see Peter's anxiety make him reckless with his words, becoming a different person to different groups to try to bring comfort to his own scared heart. But was Jesus training and equipping Peter in the room of their last supper because He knew Peter's future? Absolutely.

Thankfully, Jesus also met Peter in his fear a few days later on a beach. He didn't lay out a map for Peter's future or tell him exactly what to do every day. Nor did He tell Peter he could avoid a harsh death. But Jesus did give Peter hope. He gave His presence. He gave new life through forgiveness and grace. And He gave him a new purpose and redirected his passion to move into it.

From this moment at the end of John's Gospel onward, Peter's character shifts. His demeanor and his words carry more depth, confidence, and courage. Not because all the fear of the future is gone but because he knows the Holy Spirit will guide him. In addition, Peter's acceptance of Jesus' grace and his observance of the cross and empty tomb have led him into a deeper understanding of God's Kingdom.

---

1. Read John 13:5-17. What was Peter's posture toward Jesus at the beginning of the last supper? Why is this significant?

"Here is the promise of the gospel and the message of the whole Bible: *In Jesus Christ, we are given a friend who will always enjoy rather than refuse our presence.* This is a companion whose embrace of us does not strengthen or weaken depending on how clean or unclean, how attractive or revolting, how faithful or fickle, we presently are. The friendliness of his heart for us subjectively is as fixed and stable as is the declaration of his justification of us objectively," Pastor Dane Ortlund shares.[1]

2. Read John 13:36-38. Why do you think Jesus took the time to warn Peter of his upcoming denial?

"The denial was burnt in [Peter's] memory. When Peter preached in Acts 3, he charged [those listening] with denying Jesus (Acts 3:14). Towards the end of his life he described some dangerous men as those who denied the Lord (2 Peter 2:1)."[2]

3. Read John 18:15-18, 25-27. Where was Peter when he denied Jesus, and what was he doing?

4. How have you seen fear of the future affect your own life or the life of someone you've known?

5. Read John 21. Throughout the Gospels, Jesus offers the following invitations to His disciples and to the world:

   a. *Come and see* (John 1:39).

   b. *Come and learn* (Matthew 11:28-29).

   c. *Come and rest* (Mark 6:31).

   d. *Come and inherit* (Matthew 25:34-36).[3]

   What invitation does Jesus extend to His disciples in John 21:12, and what do you think the significance of it is?

6. What do you notice about Peter's posture toward Jesus and Jesus' posture toward Peter?

"Peter by this triple confession is restored into his former position from where he fell by his triple denial: and furthermore it is proclaimed that he is indeed a pastor, who shows his love to Christ in feeding his sheep."[4]

7. How do Jesus' words to Peter contrast with the ways our world would address this friendship?

Jesus tells Peter, "Tend My sheep." One commentator writes: "By which [Jesus] seems to intimate that it is not sufficient merely to *offer* the bread of life to the congregation of the Lord, but [Peter] must take care that the sheep be properly *collected, attended to, regulated, guided,* . . . and it appears that Peter perfectly comprehended our Lord's meaning, and saw that it was a direction given not only to *him*, and to the rest of the *disciples*, but to all their *successors* in the Christian ministry."[6]

8. The Greek word translated "feed" in John 21:15 and 21:17 (*boskō*) can also be translated "tend." Jesus was commissioning Peter to tend to His church, to "pay attention to" or "serve" it. Furthermore, a Hebrew word that is often translated "tend" could also carry the meaning "cultivate . . . 'to put through a finishing process,' 'to foster the growth of,' or 'to further or encourage.'"[5] Think of someone who has "tended" their faith well and helped give you perspective on the future. Is there anyone who does this for you now?

9. Jump ahead to Acts 4:27-29. Peter and John are boldly speaking to the Sanhedrin (judicial leaders) after receiving pushback and threats from them. In the face of what could be a fearful experience, what do they pray for?

"Prayer activates our frontal lobe, which is connected to focus and attention. This region also helps regulate our emotions and reduce our stress. . . .

"Not only does it move our bodies out of fight-or-flight mode so we can become more intentional, but it also serves as a conduit for rewiring our brains.

"[Prayer] directs us toward truth and toward a loving God."[7]

10. The fear about the future that once took over Peter's story was transformed by the Lord into bold courage as Peter shepherded believers. How do Jesus' words in John 14:15-21 give you hope and courage related to your future?

"The Holy Spirit . . . the **Spirit of truth** who will guide the disciples into all truth ([John] 16:13), will serve as **another Helper** (or 'helping Presence' . . .). He will live in Jesus' followers forever. He is Jesus' representative after Jesus ascends to heaven. The promise of the divine presence with Jesus' followers in [John] 14:15-24 includes the Spirit (vv. 15-17), Jesus (vv. 18-21), and the Father (vv. 22-24). **He dwells with you and will be in you** does not mean there was no work of the Spirit of God within believers prior to this time. . . . Rather, it indicates that the Holy Spirit 'will be in you' in a new and more powerful sense."[8]

Aubrynn Whitted prays: "You will not abandon me to these thoughts / or leave me to drown in anxiety. / You bid me come to you, / even as you draw close to me. . . . When my mind swirls / and fear consumes, / give me the endurance to keep on. / Even if the anxiety remains, / even if the worst-cases come true, / or the 'what-ifs' are proved right— / remind me that my hope is in you alone, Lord Christ."[10]

11. God will give us another Helper. The Greek word translated "Helper" in John 14:16 is *paraklētos*, which can also be translated as "Comforter." It "has the idea of someone called to help someone else, and it could refer to an advisor, a legal defender, a mediator, or to an intercessor."[9] Which of these words describing the Holy Spirit is most comforting to you today, and why?

## Your Response

What does Peter's life reveal about God's character? How do you resonate with Peter's fear and passion?

**"Lord, You know all things; You know that I love You:** Peter did believe that he loved Jesus (using the word *philio*), yet he relied on Jesus' own knowledge of **all things**. Peter understood that Jesus knew him better than he knew himself.

"Jesus didn't ask wPeter, 'Are you sorry?' nor 'Will you promise never to do that again?' Jesus challenged Peter to *love*. . . .

**"Feed My sheep:** Jesus restored Peter in the presence of the other disciples by causing him to face squarely his point of failure; *then* Jesus challenged Peter to set his eyes on the work ahead."[11]

## For Further Study

Read the following verses about the Holy Spirit and write down the descriptions given in each.

John 14:26

John 16:13

2 Corinthians 3:17

How do these passages bring hope to a world full of anxiety? What is one more verse about the Holy Spirit you could add to the list above?

# NOTES


INTRODUCTION | ANXIETY

1. KFF, "Latest Federal Data Show That Young People Are More Likely Than Older Adults to Be Experiencing Symptoms of Anxiety or Depression," news release, March 20, 2023, https://www.kff.org/mental-health/press-release/latest-federal-data-show-that-young-people-are-more-likely-than-older-adults-to-be-experiencing-symptoms-of-anxiety-or-depression.
2. Canadian Mental Health Association, BC Division, "What's the Difference Between Anxiety and an Anxiety Disorder?" HeretoHelp, accessed May 13, 2025, https://www.heretohelp.bc.ca/q-and-a/whats-the-difference-between-anxiety-and-an-anxiety-disorder.

SESSION ONE | MARTHA AND ANXIOUS CONTROL

1. See, for example, Mary Hendren, "Birth-Order Reasoning: Martha and Mary," *WomenfromtheBook* (blog), September 4, 2012, https://womenfromthebook.com/2012/09/04/birth-order-reasoning-martha-and-mary.
2. N. T. Wright, "Women's Service in the Church: The Biblical Basis," paper presented at "Men, Women, and the Church" symposium, St. John's College, Durham, England, ntwrightpage.com, September 4, 2004, https://ntwrightpage.com/2016/07/12/womens-service-in-the-church-the-biblical-basis.
3. Jennie Allen, *Untangle Your Emotions: Naming What You Feel and Knowing What to Do About It* (WaterBrook, 2024), 45.
4. Bill Gaultiere, "Breath Prayers," Soul Shepherding, accessed April 10, 2025, https://www.soulshepherding.org/breath-prayers.
5. Clare Hayns, "Martha and Mary: Attentive Hospitality," *Consider the Lilies* (blog), July 17, 2022, https://clarehayns.co.uk/2022/07/17/martha-and-mary-attentive-hospitality.
6. David Guzik, "Luke 10—The Sending of the Seventy," Enduring Word, accessed April 9, 2025, https://enduringword.com/bible-commentary/luke-10.
7. Hannah Brencher, *The Unplugged Hours: Cultivating a Life of Presence in a Digitally Connected World* (Zondervan Books, 2024), 133.

SESSION TWO | KING SAUL AND ANXIOUS ENVY

1. "The Role of Envy in Depression and Anxiety," Connolly Counselling Centre, accessed December 9, 2024, https://www.counsellor.ie/the-role-of-envy-in-depression-and-anxiety.
2. "Why Did Saul Offer Michal to David?," Bible Hub, accessed May 13, 2025, https://biblehub.com/q/why_did_saul_offer_michal_to_david.htm.
3. David Guzik, "1 Samuel 18—Conflict Between Saul and David," Enduring Word, accessed April 9, 2025, https://enduringword.com/bible-commentary/1-samuel-18.
4. "5 Things You Never Knew About Fear: Understanding the Science of Fear," Northwestern Medicine, *HealthBeat*, updated June 2025, https://www.nm.org/healthbeat/healthy-tips/emotional-health/5-things-you-never-knew-about-fear.
5. Gene Edwards, *A Tale of Three Kings: A Study in Brokenness* (Tyndale House Publishers, 1992), 11.
6. "Here's Where Jealousy Comes From (and 3 Ways to Tame It)," Cleveland Clinic, April 3, 2023, https://health.clevelandclinic.org/how-to-deal-with-jealousy.
7. Jonathan Cleveland, "Sunday School Stories: 10 Commandments | Exodus 20:1-21," sermon, 9:25, Pulpit Rock Colorado Springs, June 9, 2024, https://pulpitrock.com/sunday-school-stories-10-commandments.
8. David Guzik, "1 Timothy 6—Riches and Godliness," Enduring Word, accessed April 9, 2025, https://enduringword.com/bible-commentary/1-timothy-6.
9. John Piper, "How Could God Be Jealous?," Desiring God, February 17, 2023, https://www.desiringgod.org/interviews/how-could-god-be-jealous.
10. Tim Mackie and Aeron Sullivan, "Saul: A Tale of Self-Deception," BibleProject, March 19, 2017, https://bibleproject.com/articles/saul-tale-self-deception.

SESSION THREE | JESUS AND EMBODIED ANXIETY

1. Saugato Biswas et al., "A Curious Case of Sweating Blood," *Indian Journal of Dermatology* 58, no. 6 (2013), 478–80, https://pmc.ncbi.nlm.nih.gov/articles/PMC3827523.
2. K. J. Ramsey, *The Lord Is My Courage: Stepping Through the Shadows of Fear Toward the Voice of Love* (Zondervan Reflective, 2022), 147.
3. Walter A. Elwell and Robert W. Yarbrough, *Encountering the New Testament: A Historical and Theological Survey*, 2nd ed. (Baker Academic, 2005), 129.
4. N. T. Wright and Michael F. Bird, *The New Testament in Its World: An Introduction to the History, Literature, and Theology of the First Christians* (Zondervan Academic, 2019), 245.
5. Blue Letter Bible, "Lexicon: Strong's G4036—*perilypos*," accessed April 21, 2025, https://www.blueletterbible.org/lexicon/g4036/csb/mgnt/0-1.
6. D. A. Carson, "Matthew," in *The Expositor's Bible Commentary*, vol. 8, ed. Frank E. Gaebelein (Zondervan, 1984), 543.
7. David Guzik, "Matthew 26—Jesus' Betrayal and Arrest," Enduring Word, accessed May 20, 2025, https://enduringword.com/bible-commentary/matthew-26.
8. The Daily Grace Co., *Peace for the Anxious Heart: Bible Study on Anxiety* (The Daily Grace Co., 2024), 18.
9. Alastair Roberts, "Day of Atonement: How Yom Kippur Points to Salvation in Christ," The Gospel Coalition, October 5, 2022, https://www.thegospelcoalition.org/article/day-of-atonement.

SESSION FOUR | NAOMI AND ANXIOUS BITTERNESS

1. Seth Meyers, "How People Become Bitter and Resentful," *Psychology Today*, November 7, 2023, https://www.psychologytoday.com/us/articles/202311/how-people-become-bitter-and-resentful.
2. Meyers, "How People Become Bitter and Resentful."
3. J. D. Douglas, et al., eds., *New Bible Dictionary*, 2nd ed. (Tyndale House Publishers, 1982), 813.
4. David Guzik, "Ruth 1—Ruth's Journey," Enduring Word, accessed April 10, 2025, https://enduringword.com/bible-commentary/ruth-1.
5. Aubrey Sampson, *Known: How Believing Who God Says You Are Changes Everything* (NavPress, 2021), xviii–xix.
6. Blue Letter Bible, "Lexicon: Strong's H6395—*pālâ*," accessed April 10, 2025, https://www.blueletterbible.org/lexicon/h6395/niv/wlc/0-1.
7. "Bible Commentaries: Psalm 139," Trapp's Commentary, StudyLight.org, accessed April 10, 2025, https://www.studylight.org/commentaries/eng/jtc/psalms-139.html.
8. Blue Letter Bible, "Matthew Henry: Commentary on Exodus 15," accessed April 9, 2025, https://www.blueletterbible.org/Comm/mhc/Exd/Exd_015.cfm?a=65025.
9. Tabitha Panariso, *Loyal in His Love: An Invitation to Be Held by Jesus When Others Let You Go* (Zondervan Reflective, 2025), 125.
10. David Guzik, "Ruth 4—The Marriage of Boaz and Ruth," Enduring Word, accessed April 17, 2025, https://enduringword.com/bible-commentary/ruth-4.

SESSION FIVE | MOSES AND ANXIOUS AVOIDANCE

1. Carmen Imes, "Commissioning Moses," teacher notes, Exodus Overview class, module 1, session 5, BibleProject, accessed April 9, 2025, https://bibleproject.com/classroom/exodus-overview-carmen-imes/sessions/5.
2. These steps and the quotes under each step are taken from Eleesha Lockett, "Breaking the Cycle of Anxiety and Avoidance," Healthline, March 15, 2023, https://www.healthline.com/health/anxiety/anxiety-avoidance.
3. Jen Wilkin, *God of Deliverance: A Study of Exodus 1–18* (Lifeway Press, 2021), 53.
4. Blue Letter Bible, "ESV Global Study Bible: Footnotes for Exodus 3," accessed April 9, 2025, https://www.blueletterbible.org/esv-study-bible/notes/exo/chapter-3.
5. Kristi McLelland, *Jesus and Women: In the First Century and Now* (Lifeway Press, 2022), 23.
6. Liz Edrington, "God's Promise to Be with Us Does Not Depend on Us," Rooted, July 12, 2021, https://rootedministry.com/gods-promise-to-be-with-us-does-not-depend-on-us.
7. David Guzik, "Exodus 14—The Crossing of the Red Sea," Enduring Word, accessed April 9, 2025, https://enduringword.com/bible-commentary/exodus-14.
8. R. Alan Cole, *Exodus: An Introduction and Commentary*, vol. 2, Tyndale Old Testament Commentaries, ed. D. J. Wiseman (Inter-Varsity Press, 1973), 120.
9. Walter A. Elwell and Robert W. Yarbrough, *Encountering the New Testament: A Historical and Theological Survey*, 2nd ed. (Baker Academic, 2005), 310.
10. Madhuleena Roy Chowdhury, "The Neuroscience of Gratitude and Effects on the Brain," PositivePsychology.com, April 9, 2019, https://positivepsychology.com/neuroscience-of-gratitude.

SESSION SIX | PETER AND ANXIETY ABOUT THE FUTURE

1. Dane Ortlund, *Gentle and Lowly: The Heart of Christ for Sinners and Sufferers* (Crossway, 2020), 115.
2. David Guzik, "John 13—Jesus, the Loving Servant," Enduring Word, accessed April 17, 2025, https://enduringword.com/bible-commentary/john-13.
3. James Montgomery Boice, *The Gospel of John: An Expositional Commentary*, vol. 5 (Zondervan, 1979), 350–55.
4. Blue Letter Bible, "Geneva Bible Study Notes: Footnotes for John 21," accessed April 10, 2025, https://www.blueletterbible.org/geneva-study-bible/notes/jhn/chapter-21.
5. Blue Letter Bible, "Lexicon: Strong's G1006—*boskō*," accessed July 19, 2025, https://www.blueletterbible.org/lexicon/g1006/kjv/tr/0-1.
6. Adam Clarke, "Bible Commentaries: John 21," Clarke's Commentary, StudyLight.org, accessed April 10, 2025, https://studylight.org/commentaries/eng/acc/john-21.html.
7. Tabitha Panariso, *Loyal in His Love: An Invitation to Be Held by Jesus When Others Let You Go* (Zondervan Reflective, 2025), 187–88.
8. Blue Letter Bible, "ESV Global Bible Study: Footnotes for John 14," accessed April 10, 2025, https://www.blueletterbible.org/esv-study-bible/notes/jhn/chapter-14.
9. David Guzik, "John 14—The Departing Jesus," Enduring Word, accessed December 9, 2024, https://enduringword.com/bible-commentary/john-14.
10. Aubrynn Whitted, "A Liturgy for Those Distressed by Intrusive Thoughts," in *Every Moment Holy*, vol. 3, *The Work of the People*, ed. Douglas Kaine McKelvey (Rabbit Room Press, 2023), 250.
11. David Guzik, "John 21—The Restoration of Peter," Enduring Word, accessed April 10, 2025, https://enduringword.com/bible-commentary/john-21.

**NavPress is the book-publishing arm of The Navigators.**

Since 1933, The Navigators has helped people around the world bring hope and purpose to others in college campuses, local churches, workplaces, neighborhoods, and hard-to-reach places all over the world, face-to-face and person-by-person in an approach we call Life-to-Life® discipleship. We have committed together to know Christ, make Him known, and help others do the same.®

Would you like to join this adventure of discipleship and disciplemaking?

- Take a Digital Discipleship Journey at **navigators.org/disciplemaking**.
- Get more discipleship and disciplemaking content at **thedisciplemaker.org**.
- Find your next book, Bible, or discipleship resource at **navpress.com**.

@NavPressPublishing

@NavPress

@navpressbooks

NavPress®

CP1790